THE SPIRIT AND HIS GIFTS

THE SPIRIT
AND HIS GIFTS

The Biblical Background
of Spirit-Baptism,
Tongue-Speaking,
and Prophecy

by
George T. Montague, S.M.

PAULIST PRESS
New York/Paramus/Toronto

Library of Congress
Catalog Card Number: 74-77425

ISBN: 0-8091-1829-7

Published by Paulist Press
Editorial Office: 1865 Broadway, N.Y., N.Y. 10023
Business Office: 400 Sette Drive, Paramus, N.J. 07652

Printed and bound in the
United States of America

Contents

Contents

Preface

On August 21, 1973, at an open meeting of the Catholic Biblical Association at Immaculate Conception Seminary in Douglaston, New York, at the request of the program committee, I presented a paper entitled, "Baptism in the Spirit and Speaking in Tongues: An Appraisal." It solicited lively reaction not only from the official respondents, Fathers Martin Hopkins, O.P., and Francis Martin, but also from the other biblical scholars and the public attending, some of whom had been involved in the charismatic movement. The address was reported in the Catholic press and was subsequently published in the Winter 1973 issue of *Theology Digest*. I gratefully acknowledge the permission of that journal to incorporate here much of the material published there.

The newness of the present work consists principally in the addition of the material on prophecy, interpretation, and discernment. It is my hope that this booklet will provide a much needed bridge between my colleagues in the theological world and those Christians who, like myself, have been involved in the charismatic movement. If Christian theology may aptly be described as the verbalization

1

and discernment of Christian experience, then what is happening in the contemporary Church is of supreme interest to the theologian who is, after all, no mere curator of religious relics but rather a servant to a living and questioning community. And if, on the other hand, the ongoing Christian experience always seeks its home in the living tradition of the universal Church, then the work of responsible scholars can provide the historical and theological context for that experience and in the process perhaps help the present generation to avoid the mistakes of previous ones. This book combines the academic research and the pastoral experience of one who would like to be that scribe become a disciple of the kingdom of heaven, who can bring out of his storehouse both the new and the old (Mt. 13:52).

GEORGE T. MONTAGUE, S.M.

1
Spirit Baptism

Twentieth-century Christianity has been marked among other things by the Pentecostal revival. What began as an outgrowth of the Holiness movement of the nineteenth century spread with phenomenal rapidity in a proliferation of Pentecostal churches in the first half of this century, then entered the mainline Protestant and Anglican churches in the fifties and finally the Roman Catholic church in the late sixties.[1] Among Catholics the movement has grown more rapidly than in any of the Protestant churches, and even within the Catholic Church in America at least, more rapidly than any other movement in its history.[2] Catholics involved in the movement tend to prefer the title "charismatic," lest the experience be too closely identified with classical Pentecostalism, but Catholics as well as their Pentecostal brethren speak of their experience of the Holy Spirit as rooted in a significant moment which they refer to as "the Baptism in (or *of*) the Holy Spirit." And all point to the biblical foundations of the experience.

For the mainstream of classical Pentecostalism,

the Baptism in the Holy Spirit is the second and most significant moment of the Christian experience, essentially distinct and often in practice separated by years from water-baptism. The latter is characterized by repentance, turning to Christ and regeneration but not by the fullness of the Spirit.[3] The fullness of the Spirit comes with the Baptism of the Spirit and evidence of receiving the gift is usually expected in a charismatic manifestation, particularly glossolalia.[4] In the Catholic tradition, though the Holy Spirit has been understood to be given in Baptism, the sacrament of Confirmation has always been explained in terms of a distinct gift of the Spirit. Many of the biblical texts that have been used in the effort to establish the distinctiveness of this sacrament have also been used by the Pentecostals to support "Baptism in the Spirit" as the second and distinctive moment of full Christian initiation.[5] Though some contemporary Catholic sacramental theologians are less eager than formerly to separate the two aspects of initiation,[6] the biblical basis for Confirmation still remains a problem. And now Catholics, lacking formal scriptural teaching in their own tradition on the matter, are using the language of the Pentecostals to describe what to them has been a real and often the most meaningful spiritual experience of their lives. They call it "Baptism in the Spirit."

The purpose of the present study is three-fold: (1) To address critically the phenomenon and the term "Baptism in the Spirit" from a biblical point of view and then to relate it to the contemporary scene; (2) to discuss briefly, and again from a biblical viewpoint, the charismatic phenomenon of glossolalia with which the Pentecostal movement, willy-nilly, is often identified; (3) to discuss the associated gifts of prophecy and interpretation in a biblical and contemporary perspective.

Baptism in the Holy Spirit

The most thorough study of the first question in recent years is that of J.D.G. Dunn,[7] and an evaluation of his research is as good a springboard as any for discussing the subject. Dunn's thesis is two-fold, one directed against the Pentecostal, the other against the sacramentalist: (1) The baptism in or the gift of the Spirit "was the chief element in conversion-initiation so that only those who had thus received the Spirit could be called Christians";[8] (2) Water-baptism, which he strongly distinguishes from Spirit-baptism, symbolizes and expresses conversion and faith on the part of the neophyte; it is also the Church's acceptance of the individual into its midst, but "otherwise it is not a channel of grace, and neither the gift of the Spirit nor any of the spiritual blessings which he brings may be inferred from or ascribed to it."[9] At most, it is the occasion (certainly not the instrument) for the bestowal of the Spirit.[10]

In support of the first thesis Dunn finds his most abundant material in Paul. The most explicit text is Romans 8:9, "If anyone does not have the Spirit of Christ, he does not belong to Christ." Hence, belonging to Christ in a state in which one would not somehow possess the Spirit is unthinkable. "Romans 8:9 rules out the possibility both of a *non*-Christian possessing the Spirit and of a Christian *not* possessing the Spirit: only the reception and subsequent possession of the Spirit makes a man a Christian."[11] While Dunn does not consider what this might mean in the case of the well-disposed non-Christian[12] or of the catechumen or of the lapsed Christian, the text at least would hardly justify as normal a state of "suspended animation," as it were, between genuine initiation and a filling with the Spirit. Paul elsewhere equates the gift of the Spirit with the initial Christian experience: "Whoever is joined to the Lord becomes one spirit with him" (1 Cor 6:17). "How did you receive the Spirit? Was it through observance of the law—or through faith in what you heard? . . . After *beginning in the Spirit* . . ." (Gal 3:2f). Especially 1 Corinthians 12:13: "In one Spirit we were all . . . baptized into one body, and all have been given to drink of the one Spirit." Clearly this text makes it impossible to sustain a doctrine that membership in Christ is one thing and the Spirit-gift another.[13] Other Pauline texts move in the same direction.[14]

Titus 3:5f and John 3:5 both join *bath* (or *water*) and the *Spirit* so intimately that the two must be taken together—the work of "renewal by the Spirit" and the "birth of the Spirit" indicating the initial gift by which one is made anew or reborn.[15]

The Pentecostal doctrine rests chiefly on Acts and the apparent instances related there of chronological separation between water-baptism and the baptism of the Spirit. Pentecostals appeal to the fact that the 120 disciples were, precisely, disciples of Jesus prior to the event of Pentecost, and see in this a pattern for the two moments of Christian experience—regeneration and discipleship on the one hand, and Spirit-filling on the other.[16] Dunn is quick to point out, however, that for Luke during the public ministry only Jesus enjoys the Spirit and that even the primitive disciples do not experience genuine faith until the moment of Pentecost, which he considers the real beginning. Peter's explanation of the Cornelius incident makes this clear: "The Holy Spirit fell on them as on us *at the beginning.* . . . God gave the same gift to them as he gave to us *when we believed* in the Lord Jesus Christ" (Acts 11:15, 17). The aorist *pisteusai* (*epi*) in Acts always means the decisive act of faith by which one becomes a Christian.[17] It is interesting to note that while many instances of cures and conversions are related in Luke's gospel, there is no description of the faith-act in one or more of the intimate disciples (as there is in John 2:11, for example).[18] Luke thus seems to be consistent in withholding the meaningful faith-act till Pentecost.

In any case, even if there were a real chronological distinction in Luke's mind between genuine faith and the gift of the Spirit on the part of the 120 disciples, such a separation would not be possible for the post-Pentecostal church, for Peter's Pentecost sermon concludes with a proposition that his hearers convert, be baptized and receive the gift of the Spirit (Acts 2:28), implying a unity in the three elements of initiation with no delay in the third.[19] Thus Dunn rightly concludes: "There were no Christians (properly speaking) prior to Pentecost"[20] and "The pre-Christian experience of the 120 prior to Pentecost can *never* provide a pattern for the experience of Christians now."[21]

The anomalous situation of the mission to Samaria, where men baptized in the name of the Lord Jesus later were prayed over by the apostles Peter and John for the Holy Spirit (Acts 8:9-19) has provided Pentecostals with justification for Baptism in the Spirit and Catholics with a basis for Confirmation.[22] The text does indeed speak of the coming of the Spirit subsequent to Baptism. Embarrassed by this departure from the apparent unity of the two effects elsewhere recorded in Acts, some commentators say that here the coming of the Spirit is only in a charismatic manifestation of the Spirit already received earlier[23] or that the text refers to a second reception of the Spirit[24]—in flat contradiction of vss. 15-19. One cannot *a priori* exclude the possibility that Luke has, for his own purposes, separated what was once joined. However that may be, it is obviously Luke's intention to say that the Holy Spirit had not come upon these men in or after their baptism and that this was precisely the reason Peter and John were sent from Jerusalem—to remedy the situation. Perhaps we can detect a concern of Luke to "regulate" this Samaritan mission by incorporating it officially into the mother community in Jerusalem.[25] But it hardly seems that Luke would be making the laying on of *apostolic* hands a universal condition for receiving the Spirit, when he does not require it elsewhere.[26] Dunn's thesis is that the dispositions of the Samaritans were defective to the point of nullifying the inward effect of the initiation rite. Luke suggests this, Dunn says, by (1) amalgamating the reaction to

Philip with that to Simon, whose magic had held many spellbound, so that even Simon's baptism is followed by an infatuation with the person of Philip and the miracles; and (2) by recording that the Samaritans "believed Philip" (8:12). "They believed" (*episteusan*) is not followed here by *in* or *on the Lord* (*eis* or *epi ton kyrion*) but by "Philip" in the dative (*tō Philippō*), an indication of Luke's reservations about their commitment.[27] Thus the ministry of Peter and John was, without rebaptizing, to remove these imperfect dispositions which prevented the normal initiation rite from having its anticipated essential effect, the gift of the Spirit. Whatever the interpretation of this passage, we must at least agree with Dunn that the Samaritan situation is not considered normal by Luke, and it certainly does not provide a justification for promoting or even expecting a baptism which does not confer the Spirit.

Finally, it is the baptism of Jesus himself which provides the model for Christian initiation, and the distinctive element of Jesus' baptism over against John's (which Jesus himself nevertheless receives) is the Spirit.[28] The fact that the early Pauline letters refer back repeatedly to Christian initiation in terms of receiving the Spirit rather than to baptism merely confirms that for the early Church it was the presence and experience of the Spirit which was the most important factor in Christian initiation. This is a message which probably both Pentecostals and Catholics need to hear, for different reasons.

The Role of Water Baptism

Dunn's second thesis is that water-baptism has no essential role in Christian initiation except as a preparatory rite and at most as an expression of faith and conversion.[29] Thus, while exalting the gift of the Spirit as the essential element which makes one a Christian, Dunn consistently downplays the rite of water-baptism and removes it entirely from the realm of the Spirit. I have gleaned from his book the principal arguments in support of his thesis: (1) The opposition in Mark 1:8 between water-baptism and Spirit-baptism implies that Christian initiation is essentially preparatory to the messianic baptism in the Spirit which alone effects the entrance into the messianic age.[30] (2) The Spirit-baptism of the 120 and of Cornelius demonstrates that water-baptism has no necessary connection with the sending of the Spirit.[31] (3) The word *baptizein* does not of itself connote water-baptism but may have only a metaphorical sense as in Mark 10:38f and Luke 12:50;[32] this is the sense it has, Dunn maintains, in 1 Corinthians 12:13, where there is no question of water-baptism at all.[33] Dunn must obviously conclude that water-baptism confers neither the forgiveness of sins nor the Spirit.[34]

Let us take each of these arguments in turn. Dunn does not deny that the coming of the Spirit upon Jesus in the Jordan is the prototype of Christian initiation, but he does deny that Jesus' baptism by John had anything to do with it, and hence he flatly denies that Jesus' baptism understood as baptism in "water-and-the-Spirit" is a prototype of

Christian baptism.[35] His argument is that the fourth
gospel does not mention Jesus' baptism by John and
that the synoptics all speak of Jesus' water-baptism
as a completed act (all aorists) which precedes the
"main" action of the pericope.

But here Dunn does not adequately take account of the development of the gospel tradition
about Jesus' baptism nor of the reasons for its development. When studied in chronological sequence,
the sources reveal the early Church's progressively
greater embarrassment at Jesus' baptism by John,
with the result that the manifestation of the Spirit
gains more prominence and the role of John as baptizer is diminished. In Mark the relationship is still
quite close:"and immediately coming up" (*kai euthys
anabainōn*). Though Mark's "immediately" (*euthys*)
is not to be pressed, since it is characteristic of his
style, he has no difficulty with Jesus' baptism by
John nor with its immediate connection with the descent of the Spirit. Luke avoids mentioning John as
the baptizer and assumes that the water-rite is completed and that Jesus is praying when the Spirit de-
scends (Lk 3:21), but the present participle "praying
(*proseuchomenou*) is still tied to the preceding aorist
"baptized" (*baptisthentos*) by a co-ordinate "and"
(*kai*), which hardly justifies a strict separation of the
two moments. Matthew is even more apologetic for
Jesus' baptism by John and reports John's own pro-
test (Mt 3:14-15), yet the descent of the Spirit is still
linked in the closest sequence to the Baptism, though
clearly as the more important and climactic event.
The fourth gospel eliminates the description of Jesus'
baptism completely—though the traditional setting

for the Spirit's descent appears in the report that it was in the course of John's baptizing (mentioned twice) that he encountered Jesus. The Gospel according to the Hebrews carries this tendency even farther.[36] This progressive tendency in the sources, however, stems from Christological, not ritual or sacramental interest. An ever-greater focusing on the divine character of Jesus led to diminishing the role of the Baptist and emphasizing instead the manifestation of the Spirit and the heavenly Voice. But it really says nothing about the relationship of the Spirit-gift to the water-rite in the baptism of Christians, for whom the repentance and confessional aspect did not present the same theological difficulty as it did in the case of Jesus. That is why, though the opposition of water and Spirit is clear in the John-Jesus contrast of the early sources, in initiation texts where this Christological concern is no longer an issue, the effects of regeneration and renewal are attributed to the water as well as to the Spirit, as is most clear in John 3:5, Titus 3:5f and 1 Peter 3:21. These texts present the greatest difficulty for Dunn's thesis, not only in the importance they attribute to the water rite, which was, after all, continued by the Church, but even in the efficacy they attribute to the water.[37] The entire chapter Dunn expends trying to explain away the obvious sacramentalism of John 3:5 (pp. 183-194) is utterly unconvincing and only serves to display the increasing weakness of his position.

Concerning the Spirit-baptism of the 120, in the absence of further evidence, one must concede that John's baptism was considered adequate when completed by the reception of the Spirit—as indeed it was with Jesus. But it does not follow that the Christian water-rite necessary for the Christian initiation of all others (Acts 2:38) is only the continuation of Johannine baptism. It is the continuation rather of Jesus' baptism, which was both water and Spirit. As for Cornelius, who had experienced neither Johannine baptism nor Christian baptism, it was deemed necessary to complete the experience of receiving the Spirit by Christian baptism (Acts 10:47f), a gesture which would be utterly meaningless if it were only symbolic and forward-pointing to the Spirit, for in the presence of the reality, what further use would the symbol have?

Finally, to deprive *baptizein* used absolutely of any allusion to the rite of water-baptism is as perilous as to see it as always meaning water-baptism. If water was used in Christian baptism and the Spirit was given on that occasion, as Acts 2:38 makes abundantly clear, then it is hard to see how it could be totally absent from Paul's mind in such a key passage as 1 Corinthians 12:13, or to say that it was certainly *not* in the author's mind in the "bath of water" of Ephesians 5:26, where, countering most responsible exegetes, Dunn says: "We must go immediately from the figure of the bridal bath to the spiritual reality of the cleansing, and not via water-baptism."[38] He takes the same attitude regarding Titus 3:5f, which presents the greatest difficulty for his thesis, as he himself is forced to admit: "Of water-baptism as such there is here no mention, though it may be implicit in the thought that water-baptism, which depicts this washing, was also the occasion when it took place."[39]

In short, Dunn protests too much. In his effort to deny any sacramental efficacy to Baptism, he is forced, even in the face of such texts as Romans 6:4, John 3:5 and 1 Peter 3:21, to affirm merely symbolic and occasional causality. But, if it is para-biblical to make the biblical texts affirm sacramental instrumentality in a philosophical sense, it is just as para-biblical to make them deny it. It is indeed unfortunate that Dunn is not abreast of the best contemporary Catholic sacramental theology. The works of Schillebeeckx and Rahner, for example, are not once referred to.

Conclusions for the Contemporary Scene

The major contribution of Dunn's work, in my opinion, lies in his first thesis, the primacy of the gift of the Spirit in Christian initiation. The Spirit is not withheld for a special "second blessing" or "second moment" of the Christian experience but is necessarily there from the very beginning if Christian initiation has any meaning at all. None of the New Testament texts, even in Acts, supports the thesis of a genuine Christian initiation deprived of the Spirit. There is then, only one baptism, as Ephesians 4:5 has it, and it is the Baptism in the Spirit, not to be separated even chronologically from the water-rite as an integral part of Christian initiation. Man is born again of *water and the Spirit*.

However, it may not be as simple as all that. For the early Church, and particularly for Paul, the Holy Spirit was an experience.[40] The decline of the experiential dimension, easily documented from Church history, can be ascribed to a number of factors: the decline in the Church's eschatological self-understanding, the reaction to Montanism, which appealed to charismatic inspiration to flaunt Church authority, and the baptism and chrismation of infants for whom, obviously, the experiential aspect was minimal. Thus the Holy Spirit was more and more left to the realm of a proposition in which to believe and a sacramental sign which could "assure" his full presence. It is understandable that the Church should eventually feel that it had lost something, and the solution resorted to in the West was to capitalize on the already established separation of "Confirmation" from Baptism to stress its value as a sacrament of maturity and the appropriateness of its conferral at an age when the personal experience of the confirmand would have a greater chance. But the price for such a chronological separation was obviously the loss of something of the "initiational" aspect and the close tie with water-baptism so obvious in the New Testament. Not surprisingly we find ourselves today torn between those who want to defer Confirmation to adulthood and those who want to return to the Confirmation of infants at baptism.

Without taking sides in this controversy, I want simply to point up the problem of the experiential nature of the gift of the Holy Spirit in the New Testament and the need to re-discover this dimension. If we do not want to go the route of deferring the sacramental rites to adulthood (and I am not suggesting that we do), then there are two questions we need to resolve, one theoretical and the other practical: (1) What scriptural antecedents are there for awakening to consciousness an experience of an inward grace already conferred? and (2) What do Christians need to do to awaken this grace?

In response to the first, we have already seen that the term "Baptism in the Spirit" describes the basic Christian initiation. To apply it therefore to a later awakening experience in the already baptized (and confirmed) Christian is bound to cause confusion.[41] While Acts 2 does provide the scriptural prototype for an experience of the Spirit and for an openness to the gifts, there are other New Testament passages even in Acts, which describe an empowering or a filling with the Spirit which can happen more than once, particularly for service.[42] Of special interest is Acts 4:31, the "second Pentecost" upon the community praying with the apostles. The event has many similarities with the first coming of the Spirit in Acts 2:1-11 and would provide an acceptable antecedent for those baptized (and confirmed) Christians who experience an "infilling" of the Spirit in the context of the ministry of a praying community.[43]

An even better text, however, in my opinion is 2 Timothy 1:6f: "I remind you to rekindle the gift of God that is within you through the laying on of my hands; for God did not give us a spirit of timidity but a spirit of power and love and self-control." The gift of God in the context certainly means the Holy Spirit or some particular Spirit-gift of ministry. Obviously a gift may be ignored or neglected. In Timothy's case it needs to be rekindled, like a fire that has died to embers and needs to be fanned to flame.[44] Thus a gift long ago received may suddenly be awakened, often with a more intense experiential impact than at its first reception, like the "second conversion" experience of which the saints and mystics have spoken.

The second question is the practical one: What do Christians or the Church need to do to awaken the gift of the Spirit? Here, in discussing Confirmation, Rahner makes an important remark: "If we reflect on what the Acts of the Apostles says about confirmation, it is clear that the Spirit conferred by the imposition of hands in this sacrament is always regarded as a Spirit that manifests itself externally in the charismata."[45] This is precisely the point of the Pentecostals, and it is confirmed in the experience of Catholics involved in the charismatic movement: what makes the difference between a purely confessional faith in the Holy Spirit and the *experience* of the Holy Spirit is precisely the openness to the gifts.

2
Glossolalia

The gifts of the Spirit are obviously many. In the following two chapters I will give attention to some which appear foreign to the general Christian experience today but which are distinctive of the charismatic movement: tongues, prophecy, and interpretation.

Interpretation of New Testament glossolalia has fallen into two major categories. The more ancient view, and that still held today by some exegetes and by many conservatives, fundamentalists and Pentecostals, is that the phenomenon was one of speaking real languages, in whole or in part.[1] That the miraculous element, whatever it was, referred to speaking rather than to hearing was seen already by Gregory of Nazianzen who rejected the opposite suggestion, which few hold today.[2] Some explain the speaking as dialects of known languages rather than "foreign languages,"[3] while G.J. Sirks rationalizes the Lukan text completely in terms of the Christians spontaneously reciting various unprescribed scriptural pericopae for the liturgy of Pentecost.[4] Finally,

18

others make a radical distinction between the phenomenon of Acts, which they consider the speaking of real languages, and that of 1 Corinthians, which they do not.[5] The latter would be an example of oracular utterance requiring interpretation.[6]

The more common view today is that New Testament glossolalia in both Paul and Luke was ecstatic utterance of some kind.[7] Early twentieth-century interpreters, influenced by the nascent field of empirical psychology and also probably by the appearance of Pentecostal revivalism, described the phenomenon as unintelligible sounds produced under extreme excitement or as the "sudden breaking down of a repression in the unconscious minds of the Apostles,"[8] or the effect of frenzy and complete trance,[9] or at any rate the result of psychological abnormality.[10] According to W.D. Stacey, one of the conditions for the experience is "not too high average mentality" [*sic!*]."[11] Recent studies have indicated, however, that the contemporary experience of tongue-speaking cannot be linked to psychological abnormality,[12] and that among Catholic Pentecostals, at least, a high degree of education is the rule rather than the exception.[13] If the interpreters cited above are correct in their negative assessment of New Testament tongues, contemporary Pentecostalism is an improvement over biblical Pentecostalism!

But the biblical "ecstatic utterance" is explained by other exegetes in a way quite in keeping with extraordinary but not abnormal spiritual experience. S. Lyonnet's article, following the lead of P. Richstaetter and A. Wikenhauser, was a major contribution in this direction, particularly in the coherence he showed between the New Testament description of glossolalia and the kind of spiritual experiences of which the Christian mystics have written.[14]

But inasmuch as Luke's work may be as much as a generation later than Paul's, it will be helpful to separate our consideration of the two sources, and even in Luke, to consider Acts 2 separately from his other descriptions of the tongues phenomenon.

In 1 Corinthians 14, there is no indication either of the extraordinary nature of the gift of tongues or of its being a means of communicating in foreign languages. On the contrary, the gift and the practice of tongues appear so common Paul feels compelled to direct the attention of his audience to other gifts, especially interpretation and prophecy (14:5), and certainly the opaque nature of tongues means that it is *not* a way of more directly communicating the word to those within the community (14:2), and especially is it enigmatic to those without (14:23-25). There is not the slightest suggestion that non-believers could pick up a message in their own native language or dialect. Within the community interpretation of the oracular speech is a special gift of the Spirit (14:13) and not something automatically evident to the listener or speaker because of his acquired knowledge of human language.

Is the tongues phenomenon in 1 Corinthians, then, appropriately described as "ecstatic utterance" (Goodspeed, NEB)? This designation has the difficulty of suggesting a trance-like state or rapture. But there is not the slightest evidence in the text that the tongue-speaker is necessarily in a trance-like state or exalted beyond his control. On the contrary, those who have the gift can use it or not at will (1 Cor 14:26-28, 32-34), as Paul himself does (14:18), and can direct it to the order of the assembly for its edification (14:27, 28, 32, 40). The term "ecstatic" introduces an element which is not implied in the text and even suggests the type of impulsive behavior Paul distinguishes from that of the Spirit in 1 Corinthians 12:2-3.

What then is speaking in tongues for Paul if it is neither miraculous language nor "ecstatic speech"? 1 Corinthians 14:14 classifies it as a prayer of the *pneuma* in contrast with the *nous* which remains "empty." This suggests that it has thrust and movement without readily intelligible content. It is described as a language properly suited for speaking with God, a language expressive of mystery (14:2), primarily a prayer of praise and thanksgiving (14:18). All this suggests that the prayer is non-rational, but inasmuch as Paul expects it to be susceptible to consequent conceptualization (14:5), it would seem more precise to call it *pre-conceptual prayer.*[15] It would thus have analogies with the coming of the Spirit upon the prophet to prepare him for the Lord's word, the latter being the term of a gestational process (as, for example in Ezekiel 2:2). In the natural order, it would resemble the process of literary or artistic inspiration—the final "shape" being prepared for by a period in which the artist "feels" the creative insight building up within him.[16]

The fact that Paul is at pains to balance the use of tongues with other gifts has often led interpreters to overlook the positive values he takes for granted in the gift: (1) It is a language of genuine prayer to

God (14:2); (2) By it one builds oneself up (14:4); (3) When accompanied by interpretation its effect is the same as prophecy (14:5); (4) Paul would like all members of the community to speak in tongues (14:5); (5) Paul himself thanks God that he speaks in tongues more than any of the Corinthians (14:18); (6) Tongues are not to be forbidden (14:39); they are one of the gifts to be sought (14:1); (7) Paul is not trying to discourage tongues but merely to regulate their use.[17]

The Corinthian text would suggest, then, that the gift of tongues should be placed somewhere within the category of Christian prayer, not as an extraordinary or exceptional gift but as one that is available and desirable for all. Its advantage for personal prayer (which is not Paul's focus here) seems to be precisely in the rest it gives to the phrenetic activity of the mind—a value appreciated by the spiritual masters of all traditions,[18] and in the preparation it thus gives for a fresh experience of the word in prophecy (14:5).

Romans 8:26-27 does not mention tongues specifically, but it confirms Paul's positive evaluation of the non-rational or preconceptual moment in Christian prayer. It brings to the praying Christian the sense that he is not alone in his prayer and that somehow everything that needs to be said comes forth non-conceptually from the Spirit interceding within. Whereas 1 Corinthians 14 assumes that the prayer in tongues is praise and thanksgiving (14:18), this text envisages intercession, the expression of the eschatological longing of the Christian awaiting the fullness of redemption (Rom 8:23). It is expressed as groaning, attributed first to creation (vs. 22), then to Christians (vs. 23) and then to the Spirit (26). If tongues is in any way alluded to here, it certainly does not mean either "foreign languages" or "ecstatic utterance." Quite the contrary, it alludes to the unresolved, non-conceptual moment of Christian prayer.[19] Thus it has at least a great similarity with the similar function of tongues. It also provides a basis and justification for modern attempts to relate these forms of Christian prayer to the unconscious and to deep spiritual and even physical healing.[20] At any rate Paul in this Romans text takes for granted that the positive use of non-conceptual prayer is an experience available to all Christians.

In what sense, then, can it be called a gift or "supernatural"? Not in the sense of a miraculous intervention of Providence producing a linguistic mechanism in the speaker, but rather in the sense that the prayer is directed by faith and the Spirit to the God of Jesus Christ in filial praise or petition— and therefore in exactly the same sense that a Christian's *praying* the Our Father differs from a nonbeliever's reading it out loud. I would suggest, then, that the "divine" character of the gift comes *ex parte finis*, inasmuch as it is directed to God, and *ex parte agentis* inasmuch as it is done under the impulse of the Holy Spirit; but not *ex parte modi* as the miraculous production of unlearned human language.[21]

What then of Luke? If we consider the other references to tongues in Acts exclusive of Acts 2, we would be led to the same conclusion concerning the phenomenon as in Paul, except that the tongues experience seems to be more of the sudden and ecstatic variety, a manifestation of the overpowering impact of the Spirit first experienced (Acts 10:44-56; 19:6). But there is no indication in either of these texts of a communication in foreign languages intelligible to the hearers.

With Acts 2 the case is ostensibly different. Here Luke's compositional hand is much more evident.[22] First, the situation of the coming of the Spirit on the feast of Pentecost is properly Lukan. Although the old form of the feast involved the bringing of the first fruits to the temple, more and more the feast came to be associated with the events of Sinai, the law-giving amid cosmic phenomena.[23] Despite the persistence of the older view that this association can be dated positively only from the second century A.D.,[24] by the middle of the second century B.C. Pentecost was undoubtedly regarded, in certain circles at least, as the feast of covenant renewal, for the Book of Jubilees celebrated the giving of the Sinaitic covenant (and the Noahic and Abrahamic as well) on this feast,[25] and the annual renewal of the covenant at Qumran, where the sectarians seem to have followed the same calendar as we find in Jubilees, fell on this, the most important of their feasts.[26] Moreover, the renewal of the covenant in 2 Chronicles 15:10-12 took place in the same month as the law-giving at Sinai (Ex 19:1), and there is some basis for the suggestion that Exodus 19 was an established reading for the Feast of Weeks in the century before Christ.[27] According to rabbinical tradition, at Sinai all the nations of the earth were offered an opportunity to accept God's revelation, and Philo concurs that the giving of the Law was accompanied by signs of fire and Spirit.[28] Using motifs associated with the feast of covenant renewal[29] Luke sees in the tradition of the various groups of listeners drawn by the sound of the new community praising God (rather than preaching! 2:11) a prolepsis of the new covenant of the Spirit offered to all the nations of the earth and a reversal of Babel.[30] It is a Christian interpretation of the Jewish traditions about Pentecost.

This editorial and theological framework suggests that Luke has used the early tradition of preconceptual prayer or ecstatic praise associated with the gift of the Spirit to dramatize the address of the Spirit to all men, transcending the barriers of language. But does he mean that they were simply speaking otherwise known human languages? However much this may appear at first sight, there is a core to the tradition Luke transmits which resists this interpretation. The fact, of course, that Luke builds his account on Genesis 11:1-9 in no way implies that the Apostles were for that reason speaking languages elsewhere spoken on earth, since it may be simply a literary allusion.[31] However that may be, some of the elements of the Pentecost story can be explained only in terms of non-rational speech: (1) Only Peter does the actual preaching. If the assembled people heard preaching in native languages they understood, there would have been no need for Peter's sermon. What they heard and responded to was the community praising God in an amazing way, and it was this that needed explanation. (2) The accusation about being drunk with new wine would have no basis at all if the speakers were endowed with a brilliance in languages, but it has good basis if it is a reaction to their intoxicating joy and ecstatic outburst of praise. (3) Peter makes no attempt to explain a speaking in foreign languages but addresses himself to the accusation of drunkenness. He interprets the event as the fulfillment of Joel's prophecy. But Joel says nothing about speaking foreign languages. Ecstatic or non-rational utterance however would be covered by the verb "prophesy" in the quotation, since it is used in the LXX in that sense.[32] (4) We might add that the *necessity* of communicating intelligibly to the audience in Jerusalem was hardly the reason for tongues, for all present could have communicated in Greek or Aramaic or Hebrew. It was the superabundance of the outburst of praise, the mode of expression, that caused the amazement. If the community was engaged in ecstatic praise, it would certainly not be surprising that occasional words in the other languages known to the listeners would be heard and this, *pace* Lyonnet, without any accompanying miracle of hearing.[33] The attraction of the Jews from different lands to this sign of unity reversing Babel (and also the sneering reaction of some) provides Luke with an excellent prolepsis of the mission to the Gentiles. It is only a prolepsis, of course, since the actual going to the Gentiles is brought about in stages, particularly with the conversion of Cornelius (also accompanied by tongues!). For the time being, a certain universalism is experienced within the Jewish community itself.[34] Peter's sermon is then addressed to the "Jews, inhabitants of Jerusalem" (2:14) and the "men of Israel" (2:22).

It is hard to say exactly what is meant by the "*new* tongues" of the late Markan conclusion (Mk 16:17). There the new tongues are presented as one of the marvelous signs by which the risen Lord confirms the apostolic witness. The likelihood is that the redactor here has simply incorporated the Lukan interpretation of tongues as a positive sign to nonbelievers, but we cannot say with certainty that the text means languages comprehensible to the listeners.[35]

Conclusion

The conclusion to which this analysis leads is that the gift of tongues as reported by Paul was essentially pre-conceptual without any connotation of foreign languages. It was a laudable type of personal prayer which had entered into the community worship at Corinth and needed regulation, though not supression, there. For Luke, tongue-speaking was one of the important signs of the coming of the Spirit upon Christian converts. It appears more sudden and ecstatic than in Paul, but where Luke is more dependent upon his sources, it still suggests simply non-rational response to the gift of the Spirit rather than speaking foreign languages for the benefit of foreigners present in the audience. For the initial and primordial experience of the coming of the Spirit upon the Church, however, Luke uses a freer editorial hand. The coming of the Spirit upon the primitive disciples not only makes them burst out in ecstatic praise but also makes them *witnesses* to

Judea, Samaria, and the ends of the earth (Acts 1:8). It is not sufficient for Luke to describe this primordial event merely in terms of receiving the promise in ecstatic outburst of praise as he did with Cornelius and the disciples at Ephesus. What happened in the upper room is pregnant with promise for the nations. To highlight this dimension, Luke found the Jewish traditions about the feast of Weeks highly congenial and he used them to build upon the older tongues-tradition a fulfillment-episode to forecast the coming of the Spirit to all the peoples of the world.[36]

An understanding, then, of the layers of the tradition about tongues lends a biblical perspective to the contemporary Pentecostal experience. Although some Pentecostals would adhere strictly to "tongues" as always meaning the speaking of a human language unknown to the speaker,[37] this position is not demanded by the biblical evidence even of Acts 2, as we have seen, nor is it in fact supported by recent empirical linguistic studies of the phenomenon.[38] It seems, therefore, that occasional reports of recognition of known language-words in the sounds of the glossalalist are the exception rather than the rule, and that we are on a better track in classifying the contemporary glossolalia, like the New Testament phenomenon, as non-rational prayer or speech. To do so is not to rationalize this gift of Spirit nor to minimize the great spiritual fruits effected through it for so many Pentecostals. Nor is it meant to minimize in the least the breaking of human barriers and the leaping over chasms of alienation which the Pentecostal experience has achieved, of which Luke's report in Acts 2 would be the prototype. But it is important, if the contemporary experience is to be genuinely rooted in the biblical one, to see what is at the heart of the phenomenon and what is simply an occasional function.[39]

A final word should be said about the communitarian nature of tongues. Lyonnet's study, while seeking parallels to the "ecstatic speech" of Acts in Christian mysticism, used examples only from the personal experience of prayer. While, according to Paul, the primary function of tongues is to commune with God rather than with men, for the building up of oneself (1 Cor 14:2, 4), it is also true that he knows of a "message in tongues" spoken out in the assembly, requiring interpretation (14:5, 13). This suggests that the rhythm of pre-conceptual prayer shared openly by one member of the assembly and followed by a "conceptualizing" of the experience by another is part of the dynamic by which the community is built up (14:5). It is something therefore which the members of the community do for one another, as is the purpose of all the gifts (14:26).

3
Prophecy
and Interpretation

The popular conception of prophecy as a fore-telling of future events is an unfortunate focusing on a single and even relatively rare function of the gift. New Testament prophecy covers a wide range of forms. The whole book of Revelation is presented as prophecy (Rev 1:3); it contains hymns, visions, pre-dictions, exhortations, coded apocalyptic imagery and dense use of Old Testament motifs. In Luke prophecy covers such varied forms as ecstatic speech (Acts 2:4, 18), prediction (Acts 11:28), and spontane-ous hymn-making (Lk 1:67).

In the Old Testament prophecy is primarily a speaking forth (a forth-telling rather than a fore-telling) of the "word of the Lord" for the contem-porary situation. A prophetic message might threat-en future judgment of promise future blessings, but it might just as well be a word revealing some secret sin (as Nathan's word to David in 2 Sam 12:1-12) or condemning some public injustice (e.g. Jer 22:13-19) or interpreting the meaning of Israel's history, distant or recent (Ex 16; Is 40:2) or calling for repentance (Joel 1:13-14) or assuring Israel of the Lord's eternal love for her and his decision to forgive (Hos 1:11; Ex 16:36) or simply praising the Lord and inviting others to do so (Is 42:10-12).

What makes it prophecy is that, unlike the torah or instruction given by the priests, which derived from their knowledge of the law, or the counsel given by the wise men, which derived from life-experience, *prophecy came about by inspiration.* It had a certain unpredictability and spontaneity which the other forms of directional "input" did not have. It frequently conflicted with the cautious views of human experience and the exclusively ritual interests of the national cult. It had an element of the irrational about it which made it a constant threat to the establishment, which could just as well live without surprises. But in retrospect Israel would have to admit that the prophets of Yahweh often had more wisdom than her wise men and more religion than her priests. And she preserved the Prophetic writings along with the Torah.

In the early stages of the Old Testament prophetic phenomenon, the irruptive element manifested itself in prophetic ecstasy without verbal content. Thus when the Spirit came upon the seventy elders with Moses, "they prophesied" (Num 11:25). When Saul approached Samuel and his group of prophets he found them in the prophetic state (1 Sam 19:20). In both these cases, it was not a matter of their delivering messages from the Lord but rather of their being overwhelmed in some way by the experience of the divine presence. Similarly, in Balaam's two oracles in Numbers 24:3-9 and 15-19, the "Spirit of God" comes upon him, and there are two references to the ecstatic nature of the phenomenon (24:3f, 15-15).

The later classical prophets from the eighth century to the time of the exile had less respect for this prophetic ecstasy and never appealed to it to authenticate their ministry, for it had been abused by the prophets of Baal and others to mislead the people (1 Kgs 18:26, 28, 29). Instead, they appealed simply to the "Word of the Lord," the clear, intelligible message rooted in their firm Yahwistic faith. Ecstatic prophecy had given way to verbal prophecy. God's self-communication not only had the thrust of his Spirit. It had the shape of his Word.

And yet, the Word of Yahweh still "came" just as his Spirit had "come." It was not the conclusion of the prophet's study but of his prayer and listening (Jer 42:4, 7). It was sometimes preceded by a vision which contained the message in symbol (Jer 1:11-14), or even by a symbolic action which dramatized the meaning of the message (Jer 19). Thus, even in the classical period, there was a high respect for the non-rational or pre-conceptual element in prophetic inspiration.

This element returned in a more pronounced way with Ezekiel with whom the ecstatic element even at times approaches the bizarre (Ez 4:1-15). Finally, at the end of post-exilic prophecy, Joel predicts the return of the spirit of prophecy to the whole people (Joel 3:1), and he seems to mean the quickening, ecstatic kind of the ancient times, associated more with dreams and visions than with intelligible speech.

So in Old Testament prophecy the pendulum swings between the ecstatic, non-rational, pre-conceptual element and the intelligible, rational, spoken word. But in either case prophecy is essentially a gift of *inspiration.*

New Testament prophecy is equally a matter of inspiration. It includes not only a wide range of forms but the same dimensions of the pre-conceptual and the verbal. The Pentecost event in Acts 2 is an ecstatic, non-rational kind of experience which Peter considers the revival promised by Joel—and he calls the experience prophecy (Acts 2:18). Then Peter in his sermon interprets the events in words his hearers can understand. In 1 Corinthians 14, prophecy belongs to the stage of intelligible speech. Though prophecy as much as tongues is due to the inspiration of the Spirit, the prophet is distinct from the tongue-speaker in that he "speaks to men for their upbuilding and encouragement and consolation" (1 Cor 14:3). Thus Paul does not consider the speaking in tongues as properly prophecy. However, when tongue-speaking is followed by interpretation, it has the same effect as prophecy—the building up of the Church through intelligible speech (14:5). This suggests that Paul is aware that prophecy and tongues are related.

The relationship appears most clearly in the gift of interpretation. As already mentioned, this is not the naturally acquired talent of recognizing a foreign language but is precisely a gift of the Spirit to be sought in prayer (14:13). Does it mean that the gift is one of miraculous word-for-word translation of the sounds of the glossalalist? While this is theoretically possible, it does not seem to be demanded by the description of the phenomenon nor by the term *hermēneuein*. This Greek verb does not always mean a word-for-word translation. It can mean giving rational shape to something enigmatic, like an oracular utterance or a vision or a dream.[1] In this sense, for example, in the creation of a song the words interpret the music and the music the words. Similarly, if the "message in tongues" is pre-conceptual prayer expressive of a religious sentiment, then the interpreter who is simultaneously sharing the same basic faith experience simply intuits that sentiment and offers an intelligible "shape" or complement to it,[2] much the same as Hammerstein might supply words to a score that Rodgers has written. Plutarch's *De Musica* speaks of the performer of a musical creation as its interpreter, noting that such interpretation should extend to the mood and the feeling the composer intended.[3]

The modern difficulty of understanding this ancient view when applied to religious experience stems probably from the fact that interpretation has become a science in which the more sophisticated stages of *explanation* and *translation* have taken preeminence over the more primitive, intuitive, and experiential one of *rendering* or *performance*.[4] At any rate, the Pauline gift of interpretation would seem to belong to the more intuitive category. It would presume a common prayer experience in which the pre-conceptual dimension is voiced by one member of the community and then is given intelligible meaning by another.[5]

Inspiration and Discernment

Prophecy and interpretation, then, like tongues, have to do with inspiration. If they are all gifts of the Holy Spirit, are they therefore absolute and infallible, in the sense in which the Church has traditionally understood inspiration when applied to the scriptures? No. The picture we get of the work of inspiration in the gifts in the New Testament is quite different. Something may *seem* to be from the Spirit without being from him (1 Cor 12:1-3), and even authentic inspiration admits of degrees (1 Cor 14:29). How then can the community open itself to inspiration as a source of its life and avoid utter chaos? If the Church cannot live without the gifts, how can it live with them? We cannot conclude this study without considering the tension between inspiration and discernment. And here, as the risk of reviewing some of the evidence we have already seen, we have much to learn from biblical and early Church history.

The early Old Testament texts reveal a high respect for the numinous, the *mysterium tremendum* of the Lord God. Man's reaction in the moments of encounter is speechless awe or ecstasy. This alone, however, was soon seen to be an insufficient sign of authentic prophecy, especially when prophecy became didactic or directive (cf. 1 Kgs 18:26, 28, 29; 22:1-38), and other signs of authenticity were sought, particularly Yahwistic orthodoxy and historical fulfillment (Dt 13:2-6; 18:9-22). For this, the intelligible *word* appears as the first element of control and discernment. In the classical, pre-exilic prophets it nearly eclipses the ecstatic, pre-rational element. But in the period of the exile, which brought the death of the nation and the near extinguishing of its hopes, the ecstatic element returns in Ezekiel, who is called to re-awaken the people. Nevertheless, the *word* is still strong in Ezekiel, and a theology of the creative power of the *word* emerges with Second Isaiah toward the end of the exile.

After the return, the great work of re-establishment begins. The temple and the city walls are rebuilt, the ancient traditions are gathered, schools of scribes assemble and copy the ancient texts, legislators codify and extend the legal prescriptions, and guilds of singers are commissioned to attend to the temple liturgy. Inspiration and prophecy are not absent, but they are less spontaneous and are carefully controlled through structures. There is a preference for finding the word of God in the past traditions now available in the fixed formulations of the Torah, and study of the law becomes an ideal of the rabbis. Even what prophecy there is seems to be highly cult-centered (e.g. Haggai, Zechariah, Malachi), and there is even a polemic against free ecstaticism in Zechariah 13:2-6 with the threat of punishment by death for anyone who prophesies in the ecstatic fashion. Thus inspiration is tamed through verbalization, specialization, structure and authority.

However, under the regime of formulated traditions and the ethics of legal observance, there is also a growing awareness that the early spirit of enthusiasm is no longer moving the people. Or, as the rabbis would put it, one of the things which the first temple had and the second temple lacked was the holy spirit of prophecy.[6] In this malaise Joel prophesies that in the time of salvation the prophetic spirit will return. It will, however, no longer be the privilege of specialists but will be given in a dramatic way to all the people (Joel 3:1).

It seems fair, then, to describe Israel's attitude toward prophecy as ambivalent: she can't live with it and she can't live without it. With it, there is an abundance of life but great need for discernment. Without it, a greater external order is possible and the recourse to fixed tradition for the direction of life reduces the need for discernment—but the problem becomes precisely the fact that there is less new life to discern.

Acts and Paul

The history of Christian prophecy follows an identical pattern. The ecstatic praise recorded repeatedly in Acts is viewed as a positive sign of the fulfillment of Joel's prophecy.[7] Prophecy itself is highly regarded by Paul as an important gift for building up the Church (1 Thes 5:21; 1 Cor 14). But he too stresses that prophecy, like all the gifts, is subject to discernment and control, in a three-fold sense: (1) To the control of the prophet himself. He can stop in the midst of a prophecy, nor does he have to speak at all. He can wait if someone else is speaking, for "the spirits of the prophets are subject to the prophets" (14:30-32). (2) To the control of the authentic doctrine of the faith about Jesus (1 Cor 12:3; Rom 12:6). (3) To the discernment of other prophets in the community (1 Cor 14:29). In this sense, the gift of prophecy, while inspired, is different from the activity of the Pythia at Delphi or the priestesses of Dodona, where there were no such controls. It is of great importance to note that in the Corinthian community, where a strong central authority had not yet been established (other than Paul's at a distance), the gifts provided complementary controls of one another: tongues solicited interpretation, interpretation rendered tongues intelligible, prophecy brought a fresh meaning of the word, discernment checked the authenticity of prophecy, and so on. To what else can be ascribed the miraculous survival of this headless enthusiastic community than to the complementary interaction of the gifts of the Spirit?

Matthew

Prophets were active in the community for which Matthew wrote his gospel. In fact, Jesus himself is portrayed as the prototype of charismatic activity (Mt 4:23; 9:35) and the one who commissions his disciples to extend this activity to places where he cannot go (Mt 10:1, 7). But undiscerned prophecy has caused division in Matthew's community. That is why we find in Matthew more than in any other evangelist a warning against false prophets. In the passage about the good and the bad tree being known by their fruits, which is only a general teaching in Luke (6:43-45), Matthew makes a specific application to prophecy: "Beware of false prophets, who come to you in sheep's clothing (hence, they are outwardly Christians) but inwardly they are ravenous wolves" (Mt 7:15-20).

And Matthew does the same with other sayings of Jesus. In Luke we read, "Why do you call me 'Lord, Lord,' and not do what I tell you?" (Lk 6:46) and "Then you will begin to say, 'We ate and drank in your presence, and you taught in our streets.' But he will say, 'I tell you, I do not know where you come from; depart from me, all you workers of iniquity" (Lk 13:26-27).

But Matthew reports the same tradition with a specific application to false prophets:

"Not every one who says to me, 'Lord, Lord,' shall enter the kingdom of heaven, but he who does the will of my Father who is in heaven. On that day many will say to me, 'Lord, Lord, *did we not prophesy in your name*, and cast out demons in your name, and do many mighty works in your name?' And then will I declare to them, 'I never knew you; depart from me, you evil-doers.' " (Mt 7:21-23)

We can see in these passages Matthew's concern to provide some norms for discerning true from false prophets. One of the discerning signs is the life of the prophet. The true prophet is one who does the will of the Father, one who is a *just* man (Mt 10:40-42). We can detect here, perhaps, that some prophets in the

Matthean church were not only proclaiming teaching at variance with the words of Jesus and the church authorities but also living a life of license, hailing their charismatic activity as a sign of their authenticity and neglecting what to Matthew is the more important sign: ethical conduct.[8]

In keeping with this same preoccupation, in Matthew's gospel we find a strong warning against false prophets in the final times (Mt 24:11) and a note that as a result of false prophecy the charity of the many grows cold (Mt 24:12).

To bring prophecy within the pale of sane community growth, Matthew offers two directives: (1) A return to the words of Jesus as the touchstone of orthodoxy. Matthew, we know, gathers the oral teaching of the Jesus tradition into major discourses, and emphatically concludes his gospel with the statement that the teaching of Jesus—*all* of it—is a command that is final (Mt 28:20). These collections are not made simply out of a curator's interest but rather to provide a formulated means of discernment in a highly charismatic community. Once again, the word discerns the spirit. (2) A submission to the authority of the community leaders. This point becomes obvious when we realize the position played by the disciples of Jesus in the gospel. These disciples are the forerunners of those who are presently authorities in the Matthean community; hence what Matthew says about the disciples he is implicitly saying about the contemporary authorities. Now Matthew tends to exalt the Apostles and disciples in a way that Mark and Luke do not. They are given the power to bind and loose (18:18). Special authority is given to Peter. He is made the foundation stone of the Church (16:18). While in Mark the disciples remain completely without understanding until the resurrection of Jesus,[9] in Matthew understanding is already granted them. Though obvious throughout the gospel, this becomes especially apparent at the end of the collection of parables, when Jesus addresses his disciples:

> "Have you understood all this?" They said to him, "Yes." And he said to them, "Therefore every scribe who has been trained for the kingdom of heaven [by this Matthew understands the authentic disciple of Jesus, who is rooted in the solid teaching of the past and what is really new in the teaching of Jesus] is like a householder who brings out of his treasure what is new and what is old." (Mt 13:51-52)

Hence, while Matthew does not deny the value of authentic prophecy, it is clear that his community is moving toward measures of control in *formulation* and *authority*.

What Happened to Prophecy and Tongues?

In keeping with this trend we begin to see prophecy less as a broadly distributed gift than as an office emerging in the Church. Already in 1 Corinthians, while urging Christians to seek the gift of prophecy, Paul speaks of prophets as *placed* in the Church right after the apostles (1 Cor 12:28), that is, they have a visible, official and apparently stable role in the community. In Acts prophets become leaders (Acts 15:22, 32). According to Eph 2:20 they are, with the apostles, the foundation of the Church. In the book of Revelation the ministry of the prophet is developing, though to what extent they are a special group is not clear.[10] They are particularly hard-hit by persecution.[11] By the time of the *Didache*, prophets were held in high esteem,[12] but their number seems to be dwindling. Not every community has one.[13] They are highly welcomed in the celebration of the liturgy and are not bound by fixed formulas.[14] It is possible, though not certain, that they were celebrants of the Eucharist. The fact that they speak "in a spirit" is interpreted by some to mean in ecstasy,[15] but this designation suffers from the same vagueness we saw when applied to 1 Corinthians 14 where the same expression is used. It *could* refer, as it does in Paul, to glossolalia. It would be better, in my opinion, to translate *en pneumati* simply by "under inspiration."

The rise of Montanism in the second century marked the decline of prophecy both as a gift and as an office. What really happened in the Montanist crisis is difficult to assess because of our limited sources. Tertullian had a high respect for the Montanists and eventually went over to them himself.[16] They were not really heretics, though later contraversialists tried to brand them as such.[17] They promoted a rigorous morality and asceticism, which could at least have had the appearance of being Spirit-inspired. But the novelty in Montanus was his appeal to the non-rational and ecstatic to the extent of disclaiming any personal control in his prophetic experience.[18] As Eusebius remarks, this was contrary to the Church tradition about prophets, from the time of Paul onward. Paul had provided for certain non-rational expressions in tongues, but he distinguished these, as we saw, from prophecy and insisted that for community worship the non-rational experience should be brought to its term in conceptualization that could be discerned.

The reaction to Montanism was so strong in certain sectors that not only was its ecstaticism condemned; it was also said that Jesus himself had taught that there would be no more prophets after John.[19] Though this teaching was not universal nor was it urged by Montanus' chief opponent Meltiades,[20] the latter did say that a prophet should *not* speak in a state of ecstasy, and he saw in Montanus' strange speech a sign that it came from a false spirit.[21] While there would still be a few voices like Athenagoras and Theophilus of Antioch who respected the non-rational element in prophecy,[22] Meltiades' reactionary view did, in fact, become the prevailing mood in the Church, as Montanism was pushed out to become an obscure sect. The extreme reliance of the Montanists on the ecstatic element brought an extreme reaction of total rejection of it and a tendency thereafter to see all non-rational enthusiastic prompting as the work of the devil.[23] And this, in spite of the biblical evidence to the contrary. Greater reliance was placed on learned discourse and the development of theology with the categories of Greek philosophy.[24] Irenaeus' warning that the battle against false prophets was suppressing true prophecy was a lone voice.[25] Respect for prophecy survived only, it seems, in the veneration of the martyrs, whom Revelation (16:6; 18:24; 19:10) had named as the prophets *par excellence*.

By this time the church magisterium was beginning to solidify and a canon of authoritative scriptures was on its way to formulation. Under the impact of heresy, persecution and the delay of the parousia, there was little mood for the patient work of sifting the true from the false in a more free-floating environment such as Paul's at Corinth. What had already been perceived as control factors in Matthew's community became dominant in Church life because they were considered crucial for survival: authority and scripture.

The charism of tongues, which had provided a way of putting the community in touch non-verbally with mystery (1 Cor 14:2) now is replaced by ritual and ever richer sacramental rites, a mystery-language of symbolism. That things might go this way was already suggested by the different understanding we find in John over against Luke concerning the immediate effects of the coming of the Spirit upon the Church. In Luke, the Spirit conveys the outburst of praise in tongues (Acts 2). In John, representing a later theology, the Spirit gives regenerating power to the baptismal water (Jn 3:5), understanding of the mystery of the Eucharist (Jn 6:63) and power to forgive sins (Jn 20:22f). The movement from inspired speech (tongues?) to ritual is suggested by the puzzling statement of the *Didache* that a tested prophet is not to be questioned if he "enacts a cosmic mystery (*mystērion kosmikon*) of the church," provided he does not teach others to do the same.[26] Some following Harnack have taken the statement to mean a spiritual marriage in which Christ's relation to the Church is represented.[27] But others understand it to mean symbolic prophetic actions.[28] The latter view appears more probable in that the prophets are elsewhere given freedom with liturgical formulas which is denied to others.[29] Hence, creativity in ritual is allowed to the prophet who also has the power to speak "in the Spirit." Liturgical ritual is thus an outgrowth, in part at least, of prophecy inasmuch as the New Testament prophets, like the Old Testament ones before them, made use of symbolic actions to celebrate the eschatological mystery, just as charismatics had earlier made use of tongues to "utter mysteries in the Spirit" (1 Cor 14:2). This development is further witnessed by Chrysostom in his commentary on Romans 8:26 ("The Spirit himself intercedes for us with groans too deep for words"). Confessing his own inability to determine what Paul was referring to, he supposed that one member of the Pauline community, touched by the Spirit, had assumed the praying office for all. Then he adds: "And of this the Deacon at the present day is the symbol, when he offers up the prayers for the people."[30]

This development toward ordered ritual and authorized preaching was, in part at least, in continuity with the direction Paul already perceived as necessary for the Corinthian community. It was a way of assuring two values he was seeking: order and discernment. However, it did diminish the "authority" of the individual Christian experience, as least as a component of worship, and left all creativity of the Spirit to specialists. It put the lines between clergy and laity in bold relief, with the blessings and woes this would later bring, and it implied a practical questioning of the democratization of the Spirit-gifts apparent in Acts and Corinthians.

Prophecy, as it had been known at Corinth, was no longer considered proper for the sanctuary. More precisely, when the household-assembly model for the Church gave way to the sanctuary-and-court model, prophecy was left outside of both, except inasmuch as it might be possessed by those otherwise ordained to officiate. It did not, however, wholly die. It went instead to the arena with the martyrs, to the desert with the fathers, to the monasteries with Benedict, to the streets with Francis, to the cloisters with Teresa of Avila and John of the Cross, to the heathen with Francis Xavier. The passion felt at Corinth to share the experience of the Lord found expression in freely and privately associated groups, in religious orders and confraternities, which were eventually either condemned or approved by the Church. And without bearing the name of prophets, charismatics like Joan of Arc and Catherine of Sienna would have a profound influence on the public life of *polis* and Church. But the only acceptable form for charismatic prophets to enter the sanctuary was in their exhumed relics after canonization.

The spirit of prayer in the Church, however, was never confined to official liturgy, and the felt needs of laity and even of clerics were answered in many para-liturgical ways, of which the rosary is perhaps the best modern example. And no century would lack its reports of visions and revelations.

One of the purposes of the liturgical reform promoted by Vatican II was to provide a richer, more accessible worship for the people of God and in so doing to fulfill some of the needs which only para-liturgical rites had been meeting. In no way was the reform intended to suppress all para-liturgical piety or forms, but its provision for greater flexibility and creativity makes at least permissible the question of whether the charismatic experience today has anything to offer the public worship of the Church. I think it has, in two quite distinct ways.

First, it has provided many Christians with a radical experience of the Lordship of Jesus, of praise and of listening to the word. These are presuppositions for the liturgy. The prayer meeting, which is not yet "official" liturgy, provides a laboratory in this radical experience. It allows the spontaneity and creativity necessary to develop an involved and active faith-life through the gifts. Thus it prepares and forms worshipping Christians, and this without any need to change present structures of the official liturgy.

Secondly, some of the charismatic forms, like prophecy, may eventually find acceptance in the wider community of the Church. Anyone who has listened to the prophecies at the field Masses at the Notre Dame charismatic conferences by lay persons of the most differing backgrounds could hardly question either their orthodoxy or their appropriateness. To many their exhortatory power surpassed even the most anointed homilies. And there *was* good order, assured by the pre-selection of men and women who had "recognized word-gifts."

But most Catholic charismatics would shudder, I think, at the prospect of imposing an expectation of this kind on any liturgical assembly that was not

open to it or ready for it. The household chaos created by the sweeping liturgical changes begun after
Vatican II without adequate preparation should be a
lesson here. From a charismatic point of view, the
gifts are too precious to be used indiscriminately or
in a way that would give offense.

Conclusion

The dimension which the contemporary charismatic revival has rediscovered in the Christian experience is, it seems, its most primitive roots. The
Christian experience is basically a mystical one—
that is, a personal encounter with the Lord. It is
voiced in praise and fed by listening. Tongues is
praise and intercession in an artless, unevolved state,
having as one of its effects the preparation of the
community to listen. Prophecy and interpretation
are gifts whereby the word of the Lord comes in a
living, *now* way into the listening community. These
gifts first appeared at a time when the Church had
no other Scriptures than the Old Testament and a
need was felt to express the Christian experience in
ways that went beyond, because fulfilling, the written
text. Inspiration was the very heart of this oral
period, and complementary gifts of discernment and
service were necessary to channel native enthusiasm
into community building. As these primitive gifts
later gave way to more sophisticated Church forms,
in which discernment was already to a great extent
built in (set liturgical rites and authorized preaching), a greater assurance of order and orthodoxy was

gained, but at the price of diminishing an expectation of personal mysticism as a normal and direct contribution to the upbuilding of the community at worship. Yet such mysticism, if Christ-centered and truly Spirit-born, is the very soul of worship.

How are the charismatic gifts related to this radical experience of worship? If the history we have reviewed has anything to tell us, it is, it seems, that the free praise and word gifts which are called tongues and prophecy belong to the pre-formal or genetic roots of the Christian experience. They have much to say about what the individual and the community need to experience before formal liturgy is meaningful. This "gestational" period of prayer needs a certain freedom to be sloppy if it is to be creative, and the prayer meeting provides such freedom. To restrict the operation of the Spirit to offices and forms less open to sloppiness may assure the comfort of order, but if the *experience* released in the primitive gifts is lost, the very meaning of the forms and offices that replace them dessicates. Certainly the contemporary charismatic movement has demonstrated that for many the Christian *experience* is immensely enhanced by rediscovering those praise and word gifts in the forms which were closest to the earliest experience—tongues and prophecy.

Perhaps the broader lesson to learn from all this is that the Church needs both inspiration and discernment as much as an automobile needs both a motor and a steering wheel. Without inspiration, the Church does not move. Without discernment it does not move on course. The tension between inspiration and discernment is lifegiving, and the Church dies when it opts for one to the exclusion of the other. The future, then, of the charismatic movement in the Church will depend on how much the two poles of inspiration and discernment can be kept in creative tension. It will depend, on the one hand, on how much charismatics are willing to avoid the Montanist excess of over-emphasizing the pre-rational and how much they are open to the discernment of Church authority. On the other hand, it will also depend on how much Church authority realizes its own need to be revitalized at the roots by an ever fresh outpouring of the Spirit and his gifts. The one who, like the author of this book, is designated by ordination to preach and minister officially for the Church, must realize that beyond the theological learning of the scribe and the human experience of the wise man, there is a wisdom of the Spirit given only in prayer. And it is this inspired wisdom that moves the community more than any other. The Lord's flock has heard the theologians and the empirical researchers abundantly in recent years. What it needs now is the voice of mystics and of saints, of men and women who can give hope to the dark valley because they have been to the mountaintop. When such prophets have spoken, then the Church will rediscover its need for its wise men and its scribes and its pastors.

If, then, we must go back to our historical roots to find life, let it be far enough back, to the primitive balance Paul urged in his very first letter: "Do not quench the Spirit, do not despise prophesying, but test everything, holding fast to what is good" (1 Thes 5:21).

Notes

Chapter 1

1. For an annotated bibliography see D.W. Faupel, *The American Pentecostal Movement: A Bibliographical Essay* (Wilmore, Ky.: Asbury Theol. Seminary, 1972). For the history of the movement see the thorough study of W.J. Hollenweger, *The Pentecostals* (Minneapolis: Augsburg Publishing House, 1972). Also F.D. Bruner, *A Theology of the Holy Spirit* (Grand Rapids: Eerdmans, 1970). For the history of the movement in the Catholic Church in America see E.D. O'Connor, *The Pentecostal Movement in the Catholic Church* (Notre Dame: Ave Maria Press, 1971).

2. Accurate figures are hard to come by, but an impression of the growth can be gathered from the increasing number of prayer groups listed each year in the directories published by the Communications Center at Notre Dame (635 in 1972, 1,196 in 1973) and the growing attendance at the annual National Conference at Notre Dame (from 90 at the first conference in 1967 to some 25,000 in 1973).

3. As early as 1915 the Assemblies of God rejected the identification of rebirth and the baptism of the Spirit as a false doctrine. Cf. Hollenweger, *The Pentecostals*, 332. D.W. Basham, *A Handbook on Holy Spirit Baptism* (Reading, Berkshire: Gateway Outreach, 1969), 10. Pentecostals grant some activity of the Spirit in the first moment and some would even say that all Christians have the Holy Spirit, but they distinguish regeneration from the

"filling" by the Spirit, the latter being an empowering for service. R.M. Riggs, *The Spirit Himself* (Springfield, Mo.: Gospel Publishing House, 1949) 47f.

4. The declaration of faith of the Assemblies of God, USA, reads: "The Baptism of believers in the Holy Ghost is witnessed by the initial physical sign of speaking with other tongues . . ." Hollenweger, *Pentecostals*, 515.

5. E.g., C. Ruch, "Confirmation dans la Sainte Ecriture," *DTC* (Paris: Letouzey et Ané 1938) 3.1 (975-1026); C. McAuliffe, *Sacramental Theology* (St. Louis: B. Herder, 1958) 94f; W. Mork, *Led by the Spirit* (Milwaukee: Bruce, 1965), 99f.

6. P. Franzen, "Confirmation," *Sacramentum Mundi* (New York: Herder and Herder, 1968) 1, 405-410. K. Rahner, *The Church and the Sacraments* (New York: Herder and Herder, 1963).

7. *Baptism in the Holy Spirit* (Naperville: A. R. Allenson, 1970).

8. Dunn, *Baptism*, 4.

9. Dunn, *Baptism*, 228.

10. Dunn, *Baptism*, 157, 168.

11. Dunn, *Baptism*, 95.

12. Some theological sense must be made of those well-disposed to the good news before they hear it, like Cornelius whose moral and religious life prior to his explicit Christian experience is highly praised by Acts 10:2.

13. Dunn, *Baptism*, 128f.

14. 1 Cor 2:12; 2 Cor 3:3, 6 (the Spirit is the new covenant); 8:17 (contact with Christ = contact with his Spirit).

15. Dunn, *Baptism*, 166, 183-194.

16. Riggs, *The Spirit Himself*, 50, For other references see Dunn, *Baptism*, 39 n. 2.

17. Acts 2:44; 9:42; 16:31. Cf. Dunn, *Baptism*, 52.

18. For John, too, the Spirit is not given until Jesus is glorified (Jn 7:39). Does this mean that in his view saving faith was not possible to the disciples prior to Jesus' "exaltation"? The disciples are said to believe in him already at Cana (2:11). The problem is that John retrojects much of the Paschal "glory" into the public life of Jesus, so that

chronological distinctions so carefully guarded by Luke dissolve into typical catechesis. Hence it is extremely difficult to answer what is John's view about the relationship of faith to the activity of the Spirit *for the first disciples*. For the Johannine church, however, which stands on the other side of Jesus' exaltation, there is no question that entrance into discipleship and reception of the Spirit are simultaneous: "If anyone thirsts, let him come to me; let him drink who believes in me. Scripture has it, 'From within him rivers of living water shall flow.' (Here he was referring to the Spirit whom those that came to believe in him were to receive. There was, of course, no Spirit as yet, since Jesus had not yet been glorified.)"

19. The future *lēmpsesthe* of Acts 2:38 is not a dilatory future but the future of unqualified promise, to be fulfilled immediately upon the conditions preceding. Cf. Dunn, *Baptism*, 91, *contra* J.D. Stiles, *The Gift of the Holy Spirit* (Old Tappan, N.J.: Fleming H. Revell, 1971), 8, and M.C. Harper, *Power for the Body of Christ* (London: Fountain Trust, 1964), 25.

20. Dunn, *Baptism*, 51. The case of the Virgin Mary would seem to be an exception, in the light of what Luke says of her in 1:45, and implicitly in 1:38 and 11:28. But the exception is precisely that her personal Pentecost was anticipated in order that the child might be conceived (1:35) and also, most probably, if we follow the parallel of Luke with Acts, that she might be a prototype of the believing (Lk 1:45; Acts 11:15, 17) and Spirit-filled (Lk 1:35; Acts 2:1-11) community. But see also Lk 1:15, 41, 67; 2:25.

21. Dunn, *Baptism*, 53.

22. D. Basham, *Handbook*, 15f, 17. Other references in Dunn, *Baptism*, 59 n. 1. Official usage of this text in support of Confirmation goes back at least to Pope Innocent I and is found in Peter Lombard. Cf. K. McDonnell, *The Baptism in the Holy Spirit as an Ecumenical Problem* (Notre Dame: Charismatic Renewal Services, 1972). Catholic usage of this text is still found in the respected scholar B. Neunheuser, *Baptism and Confirmation*,

trans. J.J. Hughes (New York: Herder and Herder, 1964), 47f.

23. G.R. Beasley-Murray, *Baptism in the New Testament* (London: Macmillan, 1962), 199; J.E.L. Oulton, "The Holy Spirit, Baptism, and Laying on of Hands in Acts," *ExpT* 66 (1954-55) 238f.

24. Riggs, *The Spirit Himself*, 52; P.T. Camelot, "Confirmation," *NCE* IV, 145.

25. J. Fitzmyer, *JBC*, *ad loc.*; E. Haenchen, *The Acts of the Apostles* (Philadelphia: Westminster, 1971), 306. Further references in Dunn, *Baptism*, 58, n. 14.

26. Catholics have pressed Acts 8 to imply that the imposition of hands was reserved to the Apostles (e.g. P.T. Camelot, "Confirmation," 145; Neunheuser, *Baptism*, 44), but Luke could hardly have been making this point and then go on at once to relate the conversion and water-baptism of the eunuch by the same unqualified Philip (Dunn, *Baptism*, 58), particularly since we may assume that the eunuch also received the Holy Spirit, as the Western Text says explicitly. Ananias likewise had no apostolic status in praying over Paul. To argue, as both Camelot and Neunheuser do, on the basis of 1 Cor 1:17 that Acts 19 means Paul did not baptize those on whom he laid hands is groundless on the basis of 1 Cor 1:16.

27. Dunn, *Baptism*, 65.

28. Already in Mark the linking concept in 1:1-13 is the thrice-mentioned *Spirit*. Luke, of course, develops it more extensively. Some Pentecostals compare the conception and birth of Jesus on the one hand, and his later anointing by the Spirit at his baptism thirty years later to the two moments of the Christian life—regeneration and baptism in the Spirit, the latter being anointing for service. Though there is much to support this interpretation, the central thrust of the baptismal narration is not the personal experience of Jesus but the moment of ushering in the messianic age and Jesus into the messianic age.

29. Dunn, *Baptism*, 219, 227, 228.

30. Dunn, *Baptism*, 18f. "If, as seems most likely, the Christian practice of water-baptism from the first was sim-

ply a continuation and adaptation of the Johannine rite,
and if, as also seems most likely, Jesus' own baptism was
seen as the pattern, then it should be noted that the essentially preparatory nature of the Johannine baptism was
carried over into Christian baptism . . . the water-baptism
itself does not effect entrance into the new age and Christian experience but only points forward and leads up to the
messianic baptism in the Spirit which alone effects that entrance." Dunn, *Baptism*, 99. "Christian water-baptism
takes the place of John's water-baptism as symbol of and
contrast with Christ's Spirit-baptism." Dunn, *Baptism*, 20.

31. Dunn, *Baptism*, 18, n. 38, 100.

32. Dunn, *Baptism*, 18.

33. Dunn, *Baptism*, 129. He similarly denies that
"you were washed" in 1 Cor 2:12 alludes in any way to
water-baptism.

34. Dunn, *Baptism*, 97, 99.

35. Dunn, *Baptism*, 33.

36. Cf. Jerome, *Contra Pelag.* III, 2.

37. The *dia tou baptismatos* of Rom 6:4 certainly
gives the rite some efficacy, as Dunn is forced to admit,
145, cf. also 154.

38. Dunn, *Baptism*, 163.

39. Dunn, *Baptism*, 168. Italics mine.

40. Acts 2:4; 4:31; 9:31; 10:44-56; 13:52; 19:6; Rom
5:5; 8:1-16; 1 Cor 12:7, 13; 2 Cor 3:6; 5:5; Gal 4:6; 5:16,
18, 25; 1 Thes 1:5f; Tit 3:6; Jn 3:8; 4:14; 7:38f; 16:7.

41. Even Acts does not call any of the subsequent
"comings" of the Spirit "baptism." If we cannot find a
better term for the "awakening" experience than "Baptism
in the Spirit," then it is important to keep in mind the distinctions between such an experience and the sacraments
of Baptism and Confirmation, as explained well by D.
Gelpi, *Pentecostalism: A Theological Viewpoint* (New
York: Paulist Press, 1971) 177-186.

42. Acts 2:4; 4:8, 31; 9:17; 13:9; Eph 5:18.

43. Because the classical Pentecostals before them
used the term "Baptism in the Holy Spirit" to describe the
profound initiation into new life in the Spirit, Catholics

naturally were led to seek an explanation of the experience in their baptismal grace. All grace is, according to Catholic theology, in some way sacramental, but that does not mean every grace must be manifestly and directly connected with the reception of a sacrament. As is clear from the New Testament, significant new departures of the Spirit are given simply in the context of prayer. Thus, despite Catholic predisposition to connect any significant departure in the Christian life to some sacrament, the new experience of the Spirit, even though a powerful new beginning, may be adequately explained as a prayer-experience or, in Thomistic terms, as the divine indwelling which always supposes an *innovatio* in the spiritual life. (I am indebted for this insight to Father Frank Sullivan, S.J., of the Gregorian University, Rome, in an excellent paper presented at a theological conference at Notre Dame July 22, 1973. I can only hope for the paper's early publication.)

44. The first chapters of Revelation are concerned with re-conversion of Christian communities and could thus provide another model. However, the "Baptism in the Spirit" is often experienced by Christians who have previously led exemplary lives, and so the texts of filling or empowering or rekindling for service seem more appropriate than these re-conversion texts.

45. *The Church and the Sacraments*, 90. Augustine already noted with regret that in his day the imposition of hands by the bishop no longer seemed to release the charisms as in the early Church. *De Bapt.* III, 16, 21.

Chapter 2

1. This was the interpretation of Irenaeus (*Adv. Haer.* V, vi, 1) and Chrysostom (*Hom.* xxix on 1 Cor 12:1-11). Among moderns, J.G. Davies, "Pentecost and Glossolalia," *JTS* 17 (1966) 299-307. Even F. Prat, who recognized that the gift was one of prayer rather than preaching, held that it was utterance of human languages. *Théologie de St. Paul* (Paris: Beauchesne, 1961) 1, 153.

2. Cf. M. Kelsey, *Tongue-Speaking, An Experiment in Spiritual Experience* (New York: Doubleday, 1964) 150.

3. H.E. Edwards, "The Tongues at Pentecost, a Suggestion," *Theology* 16 (1928), 248-252.

4. G.J. Sirks, "The Cinderella of Theology," *HTR* 50, (1957), 77-89. This view is accepted by C.S. Mann in J. Munck's *The Acts of the Apostles* (New York: Doubleday, 1967), 275. That the event was principally a reciting of scripture texts was already suggested by R.O.P. Taylor, "The Tongues at Pentecost," *ExpT* 40 (1928-29), 300-303.

5. So most moderns at least as they read the intention of Luke in contrast with Paul. That there is a profound difference between the two events was already pointed out by D. Brown, "The Acts of the Apostles, chap. 2, The Day of Pentecost," *Expositor* Series 1, Vol. 1 (1875), 397.

6. S.D. Currie, " 'Speaking in Tongues': Early Evidence Outside the New Testament Bearing on 'Glossais Lalein,' " *Int* 19 (1965), 274-294.

7. Thus the NEB translates simply, "ecstatic utterance."

8. L. Dewar, "The Problem of Pentecost," *Theology* 9 (1924), 250.

9. W.S. Thomson, "Tongues at Pentecost, Acts 2," *ExpT* 38 (1926-27), 284-286.

10. I.J. Martin, "Glossolalia in the Apostolic Church," *JBL* 63 (1944), 123-130, who says that by the Aramaic address Peter finally "saved the day" for the Church that otherwise would have suffered reproach and misunderstanding! (128) E. Lombard's even more critical view (*De la glossolalie chez les premiers chrétiens*, Lausanne, 1910) is answered by R.P.J. Renié, *Actes des Apôtres* (Paris: Letouzey et Ané, 1951), 55.

11. W.D. Stacey, "Tongues," *Hastings Dict. Bibl.*, Rev. Ed., (New York: Scribners, 1963) 1008.

12. J.P. Kildahl, *The Psychology of Speaking in Tongues* (New York: Harper and Row, 1972); F.D. Goodman, *Speaking in Tongues: A Cross-Cultural Study of Glossolalia* (U. of Chicago Press, 1972). Cf. V.H. Hine,

"Pentecostal Glossolalia: Toward a Functional Interpretation," *JSSR* 8 (1969), 211-226: ". . . there is no evidence
. . . that the differences . . . found indicate abnormality
or psychological pathology of any kind. . . . Quite clearly,
available evidence requires that an explanation of glossolalia as pathological must be discarded." Also M. Kelsey, *Tongue-Speaking*, 146-147, who also (204f) refers to
the then yet unpublished thesis done for the psychiatry
department of the University of Johannesburg, South
Africa, by Dr. L.M. van Vivier, who reached the same
conclusions. See now his published "The Glossolaic and
his Personality" in *Beiträge zur Ekstase*. Theodor Spoerri,
ed. Bibliotheca Psychiatrica et Neurologica N. 134 (Basel:
S. Karger, 1968).

13. Preliminary results of a yet unpublished survey by
Loyola University of New Orleans, 1973.

14. P. Richstaetter, *Scholastik* 11 (1936), 321-345; A.
Wikenhauser, *Die Apostelgeschichte* (Regensberger N.T.
5, 1936). S. Lyonnet, "*De Glossolalia Pentecostes eiusque
significatione*," *VD* 24 (1944), 65-75. English translations
of the passages to which Lyonnet refers are herewith given
with thanks to Dr. J.M. Ford, *Baptism of the Spirit*
(Techny, Ill.: Divine Word, 1971). St. Teresa, *Life*, 16:
"Then the soul does not know what it should do, whether
to speak or be silent, laugh or cry . . . Then many words
are pronounced in praise of God, yet without order, unless
God himself gives the order; however, the human mind can
do nothing." St. Bernard of Clairvaux, *In Cant.* 67:3 (PL
183, 1003f): "Thus love, especially divine love, is strong
and burning, when it is not able to restrain itself within itself, it does not wait for any order . . . it overflows because of poverty of words, while it feels no loss to itself
through this. Meanwhile it requires neither words nor
voice, content alone with sighs." St. Alphonsus, *Homo
Apostolicus*, Appendix 1, 15: "Spiritual intoxication
causes the soul to break forth in, as it were, delirium, such
as songs cries, immoderate weeping, leaping et cetera, as it
used to happen to St. Mary Magdalen of Pazzi."

15. Obviously, "pre-conceptual prayer" is a generic

classification also applicable to other forms of prayer, and so I am not suggesting that the term be used as a translation for the specific kind of prayer described in the NT *glossais* passages. These should, in my opinion, be rendered not by "foreign languages" nor by "ecstatic utterance" (even less by the crude and impersonal "strange sounds" of *Today's English Version*) but by the usual "speaking (or praying) in tongues."

16. That musical inspiration has much to say about the gift of prophecy is implied in the fact that the Chronicler sees in the singers of the post-exilic temple the successors of the pre-exilic prophets or at least of those ancient singers "who used to prophesy" (1 Chr 25:2, 3), one of whom was the "seer" of the King (25:5). Luke calls Zechariah's on-the-spot composition of his canticle an act of prophecy (Lk 1:67), and Paul refers more than once to hymns and inspired singing (Col 3:16; Eph 5:18f), especially in his directions to the Corinthian charismatics (1 Cor 14:15, 26), where "singing with my spirit" is clearly one of the ways of praying in tongues, to be accompanied or followed, Paul hopes, by "singing with my mind as well" (14:14f).

17. Beare's position ("Speaking," 243) that Paul is trying to *discourage* their use founders on 14:39.

18. Prayer in tongues has many similarities, I think, with the Jesus-prayer of the Hesychast tradition.

19. Paul does not call for or expect an interpretation of the non-conceptual prayer here as he does in 1 Cor, and he is also much more positive in his assessment of it. Thus we get an idea of how Paul felt about the value of this kind of "prayer in the Spirit" when his view was not limited by his reaction to the immediate abuses in Corinth.

20. See M. Kelsey, *Tongue-Speaking*; also his *Healing and Christianity* (N.Y.: Harper and Row, 1972). Many charismatics speak of the healing and liberating experience that has come to them through yielding to tongues. In Jungian terminology the unshaped and chaotic forces of the unconscious (even of "the shadow") have been tapped and integrated.

21. I am fully aware that in contemporary Pentecostal experience there are instances related of surprising communication in the language of the hearer unknown to the tongue-speaker. In such cases an especially fortuitous act of Providence may have been at work, but this would be by way of added grace not generally associated with tongue-speaking. Paul at least makes no provision in 1 Cor 14 for such occurrences.

22. This is true also of the way Luke presents Peter's Pentecost sermon in Acts 2 when studied against his reporting of the sermon in Acts 3. Cf. R. Zehnle, *Peter's Pentecost Discourse, SBLMS* 15 (Nashville: Abingdon Press, 1971).

23. Cf. W.L. Knox, *The Acts of the Apostles* (Cambridge U. Press, 1948), 84.

24. S. Maclean Gilmour, "Easter and Pentecost," *JBL* 81, (1962), 66; J.C. Rylaarsdam, "Feast of Weeks," *IDB* (1962) IV, 828.

25. *Jubilees* 6:14-21; 15:1-24.

26. I QS 1, 2. R.K. Harrison, "The Rites and Customs of the Qumran Sect," in *The Scrolls and Christianity,* ed. M. Black, (London: SPCK 1969), 34; R. de Vaux, *Ancient Israel* (New York: McGraw-Hill, 1961), 494. The Qumran community had a developed theology of the "Holy Spirit." Thus the covenanter could say, "I know that with thy good pleasure I have a part in thy holy Spirit" (IQH 14:13), he could speak of the holy Spirit coming upon him (IQH 7:6). In the final time, God would cleanse all the acts of man by his holy spirit, pouring out the spirit of truth like lustral waters (IQH 4:21).

27. Based on the Talmudic tradition, *Meq.* 31s. N. Adler, "Pfingsten," *LTK* 8 (1963), 421; R.K. Harrison, "Rites," 34.

28. *Midrash Raba* on Ex 22:9. Philo, *de Decalogo*, 33-35: "The ten words . . . were delivered by the Father of All when the nations . . . were assembled together. Did he do so by his own utterance in the form of a voice? Surely not: . . . God is not as a man needing mouth and tongue and windpipe. I should suppose that God wrought

on this occasion a miracle of a truly holy kind by bidding an invisible sound to be created in the air more marvelous than all instruments and fitted with perfect harmonies . . . which giving shape and tension to the air and changing it to a *flaming fire*, sounded forth like the *breath* (*pneuma*) through a trumpet an articulate voice so loud that it appeared to be equally audible to the farthest as well as the nearest. . . . The new miraculous voice was set in action and *kept in flame* by the power of God which breathed upon it (*epipneousa*) and spread it abroad on every side and made it more illuminating in its ending than in its beginning by creating in the souls of each and all another kind of hearing far superior to the hearing of the ears." Cf. also *Spec. Leg.* II, 189.

29. With Kutschmar, Kutsch, Haenchen, Reicke, Adler (*LKT* 8 (1963). 421). Contra R. de Vaux, *Ancient Israel*, 495. The fact that the conservative rabbis accepted the Feast of Weeks as a commemoration of the Law-giving at Sinai only in the second century A.D. does not negate its presence in other circles much earlier.

30. E.G. King, "The Influence of the Triennial Cycle upon the Psalter," *JTS* 5 (1904), 203-213, already pointed out the relationship of Pentecost to the account of Babel according to the triennial cycle of readings prescribed for the synagogue. The first year of the cycle began on Nisan 1, and the opening verses of Genesis were then read. The eleventh chapter would have fallen on the Feast of Weeks, narrating the story of Babel, i.e., the confusion of tongues. The gift of the Spirit is the reversal of Babel. Cf. I. Abrahams, *Studies in Pharisaism and the Gospels* (New York: K.T.A.V., 1967), 10. The theme of Pentecost as a reversal of Babel is a favorite of the Fathers: Chrysostom, *Serm. 2a in Pent.* (*PG* 50, 467); Augustine, *Serm.* 271 (*PL* 38, 1945); Bede, *Super Act. Apost. expositio* (*PL* 92, 947; Thomas Aquinas, *Summa Th.,* II-II, q. 176. a. 1.

31. Gundry rightly criticizes Davies on this point; cf. n. 4 above.

32. Num 11:25, 26, 27 (29); 1 Sam 19:20, 21, 23, 24. Cf. E. Haenchen. *Acts*, 178, 185.

33. Lyonnet considers the miracle one of hearing as well as speaking, on the force of the text of v. 8 and v. 11, that each listener heard each speaker speaking the listener's language (*De Gloss.*, 71). I fail to see this interpretation as necessary.

34. As already in the infancy narratives, Lk 2:31f, and Luke's gospel *passim*. Luke's thought moves in two directions: on the one hand he wishes to extend the benefit of the event to as many nations as possible; on the other, he is aware that the mission to the Gentiles actually occurred later. The tension he sees resolved in the fact that all those drawn to the event were Jews yet representing the nations. Thus it does not matter greatly whether these men were diaspora Jews who had immigrated to Palestine (F.W. Beare, "Speaking With Tongues: A Critical Survey of the N.T. Evidence," *JBL* 83 (1964), 237) or whether they had just come for the feast to join the "inhabitants of Jerusalem" (v. 14).

35. Already in Paul (1 Cor 14:22) tongues are presented as a sign to non-believers but the meaning is clearly a non-efficacious sign (14:21, 23). The apparently contradictory roles assigned to prophecy in 14:22 and 23-25 may be explained by the fact that Paul does not put prophecy in the category of sign. One should note the absence of *sēmeion* in the second member the parallelism of v. 22 and not supply it gratuitously in the translation: "Hence, tongues are a sign not to believers but to non-believers, whereas prophecy is not for non-believers but for believers." That is, the meaning of tongues as a legitimate prayer of praise is clear to believers who have experienced the Spirit, whereas this meaning is not readily apparent to visiting non-believers. Prophecy, on the other hand, has less of the opaque ("sign") about it, and although its purpose is the upbuilding of the believing community and not for preaching to outsiders, it is nevertheless intelligible to both groups, whence its superiority.

36. It is extremely difficult to determine to what extent the situating of the Spirit-gift on the feast of Pen-

tecost depends on pre-Lukan *Christian* tradition. In attributing the gift of the Spirit, along with the charisms, to the risen Lord Luke is, of course, at one with Paul and John. That the manifest moment at which this took place could have been the celebration of the feast of Pentecost is certainly historically as probable as that it took place on Easter Sunday (Jn. 20:22), since the viewpoints of the two reports are different. John's concern is to root the sacramental life of the Church in the Spirit-gift of the risen Lord whereas Luke focuses on the explosive charismatic manifestation of the same gift. The least that can be said is that the Christian linking of the Jewish Pentecost traditions with the gift of the Spirit is probably pre-Lukan. Whether this was a connection that was seen only in time by the reflecting community or whether the connection was suggested by what was actually experienced on the first Pentecost after the Resurrection we have no control-sources for establishing other than the text of Acts which clearly intends to affirm the second of the two alternatives.

37. Charles Parham, with whom classical Pentecostalism began at the turn of the century, apparently was so convinced that this was the case that he began to teach that missionaries would no longer be compelled to study foreign languages to preach in the mission fields. Though very few Pentecostal leaders accepted this conclusion, Parham held it until his death. V. Synan, *The Holiness-Pentecostal Movement* (Grand Rapids: Eerdmans, 1971), 102f.

38. Linguistic studies of the phenomenon of tongues indicate that generally it does not correspond to known human languages. Cf. W.J. Samarin, *Tongues of Men and of Angels* (New York: Macmillan, 1972); F.D. Goodman, "Phonetic Analysis of Glossolalia in Four Cultural Settings," *JSSR* 8 (1969), 277-339.

39. This is not to deny that Luke intends to describe the function of tongues on Pentecost as miraculous communication. Nor is it to deny occasional parallels reported in Pentecostal experiences. It is simply to show that the

mainstream of the tongues tradition is non-rational speech or pre-conceptual prayer and that this element is to be found even in the miraculous communication story of Acts 2. For a respected Pentecostal who supports this general view of glossolalia cf. D. Gee, *Concerning Spiritual Gifts* (Springfield, Mo.: Gospel Publishing House, 1972) 62f.

Chapter 3

1. Especially in Plato and Philo. Cf. J. Behm, *TDNT* 2, 664f.

2. J. Behm, *TDNT* 2, 665. The insistence that interpretation is miraculous translation can lead to the kind of reaction reported by J.P. Kildahl, *Psychology*, 63. A man raised in Africa attending a prayer meeting at which he was a complete stranger rose and spoke the Lord's Prayer in the African dialect he had learned in his youth. Another person "interpreted" the message as referring to the imminent second coming of Christ. Kildahl uses this example implicitly but appropriately to dismiss "interpretation" as specific translation. What he does not perhaps realize is that the Lord's Prayer itself is a heavily eschatological petition for the coming of the kingdom. Cf. R.E. Brown, "The Pater Noster as Eschatological Prayer," *TS* 22 (1961). Taking interpretation in the sense we have used it, there could hardly have been a better response to this prayer than an assurance that the kingdom is indeed coming soon.

3. Plutarch, *De Musica* ii, 1144 E.

4. Cf. R.E. Palmer, *Hermeneutics* (Evanston: Northwestern University Press, 1969), 13-32.

5. Sometimes the interpretation can be given by the speaker himself (1 Cor 14:5).

6. b. Yoma 21b; Num. Rabba 15:10. Cf. W.D. Davies, *Paul and Rabbinic Judaism* (London: S.P.C.K., 1958), 208-212.

7. Acts 2:4, 17; 4:31; 10:44 ff; 11:15; 19:6.

8. The *Didache* distinguishes the false prophet from

the true one on the basis of conduct (11:10). The true prophet is not self-seeking (11:9; 11:12; 16:3). The Hermetic literature pursues this in even greater detail (m. 11).

9. Mk 4:13; 6:5 1f; 7:18; 8:17-21; 9:6, 10, 32; 10:32.

10. G. Friedrich, *TDNT* 6, 850, interprets Rev 11:18; 16:6; 18:24 as implying a distinction and primacy given to the prophets over the ordinary "saints." But the expression "the blood of prophets and of saints," rather than distinguishing two classes, reflects the author's affection for the epexegetic "and" (as in 17:6, "the blood of the saints and the blood of the martyrs," which are two ways of saying the same thing). So E. Schweizer, *Church Order in the New Testament* (London: SCM, 1961), 134, n. 491.

11. Rev 16:6; 18:24. One interpretation of Rev 19:10d is that the spirit of prophecy manifests itself in the martyrs. In the light of the *other* texts of Revelation which associate shedding of blood with prophecy, this is possible. But in the light of the immediate context forbidding angel worship, the direct sense is rather that the spirit of prophecy proves its authenticity by proclaiming Jesus as Lord (as in 1 Cor 12:3).

12. *Didache* 11:7; 13:1-7.

13. *Didache* 13:4. This is surprising in view of the fact that the term "office" replaces that of "charism" for the function of the prophets as much as for that of the bishops and the deacons. Cf. E. Schweizer, *Church Order*, 142-143. Apparently a prophet could not be had by mere ordination or appointment.

14. *Didache* 10:7.

15. E. Schweizer, *Church Order*, 143.

16. *De Anima* 9, *CSEL* 20, 310.

17. Hippolytus, *Philos*. viii, 19; x, 26; Cyprina, *Ep*. 55:7.

18. Eusebius, *Eccl. Hist*. V, 16, 7-9; Epiphanius, *Pan*. 48:4.

19. Filastrius, *De haer*. 78 (*CSEL* 38, 40).

20. "The apostle grants that the prophetic gift shall be in all the church until the final coming." Meltiades as quoted by Eusebius, *Eccl. Hist*. V, 17, 4.

21. Eusebius, *Eccl. Hist.* V, 16, 7-9.

22. Athenagoras, *Embassy*, 9, speaks explicitly of prophetic ecstasy; cf. also Theophilus of Antioch, *Ad Aut.* II, 9.

23. Not in every aspect, however. Respect for dreams as a medium for occasional divine communication continued to be widespread even among those of the most orthodox Christian tradition. But beneficent dreams were generally understood to concern only the individual's private life. Cf. M.T. Kelsey, *Dreams: The Dark Speech of the Spirit* (New York: Doubleday, 1968), 102-163.

24. H. von Campenhausen, *Ecclesiastical Authority and Spiritual Power in the Church of the First Three Centuries* (Stanford Univ. Press, 1969), 191. P. de Labriolle, *La crise moderniste* (Paris: E. Laroux, 1913), 567.

25. *Adv. Haer.* III, 11, 9.

26. *Didache* 11:11

27. E. Schweizer, *Church Order*, 143.

28. J.P. Audet, *La Didaché* (Paris: Gabalda, 1958) 451f.

29. *Didache* 10:7

30. *Hom.* XIV, *ad loc.*